THE ULTIMATE
LEADERSHIP
WORKBOOK

Eric Jackier

© Eric Jackier 2019

The Ultimate Leadership Workbook

Copyright © 2019 by Eric Jackier

All Rights Reserved

Cover and art design
By
Write My Wrongs Self-Publishing

No part of this book may be reproduced, stored in a retrieval system, or transmitted by any means, electronic, mechanical, photocopying, recording or otherwise without written permission from the author

www.jtdcoaching.com

ACKNOWLEDGEMENTS

Mom and Dad for making it all possible.

Mkada, my friend, partner and co-author of the Art of Mentoring. Your support has been amazing. I'm forever grateful.

Ann Babiarz, my coach. JTD would be a lot different, as would my career if it weren't for you. Thank You!

Brian Tracy and Jack Canfield, for your support and for putting me on my path to true success.

Lynn Guerin and Craig Impelman, for hosting a wonderful week in Los Angeles and bringing the teaching of Coach John Wooden to life. Not to mention tolerating my awful performance on the court.

Danielle S, Madison D, and James L, my wonderful and patient editors from Write My Wrongs. Thanks for your help!

And especially to all the leaders of their businesses. I wish you all the success in the world!

The Ultimate Leadership Workbook

CONTENTS

About the Author	7
Introduction	9
The Benefits of Coaching	11
My Process of Becoming a Professional Speaker, Trainer, and Coach	14
You are a Professional, But are you a Good Leader for your Business?	18
The Critical Difference Between Coaching and Mentoring, and the Value Each Provides to a Business Owner	20
The Foundation of Leadership Excellence	25
Analyzing Yourself as a Leader	32
The Daily Challenges of Leadership	36
Using Your Enhanced Leadership Tools to Develop Your Company to its Full Potential	41
The Plan For Growth	45
An Essential Leadership Skill: Effective Communication	50
Leading Your Employees	54
The Value of Mentoring as Part of Leadership	57
Setting the Tone for Success	62
Leading the Heart of the Business: Your Clients	67
Conclusion: Now You See Why This is a Workbook	75
Notes	77

ABOUT THE AUTHOR

Eric Jackier is a professionally trained and certified speaker, trainer, and coach who teaches leadership and mentoring at the highest level by studying the great leaders of history, business, and sports—past and present.

As the Chair of the Disability Mentoring Day Program of NYC for ten years, he has brought high quality leadership and mentoring to a population of people who can benefit from someone who believes in their capabilities.

As a person who has cerebral palsy and has had to find his own way to step outside of what people believe is possible for those who are disabled, Eric knows firsthand that all things are possible.

He is inspirational proof that anyone can rise and become a leader in their own right with a solid system of support through mentoring and leadership training.

www.jtdcoaching.com

Certifications

Executive Director, The John Maxwell Team
Certified Trainer, Jack Canfield
Member and Certified Coach, International Coach Federation
The Brian Tracy Speaking Academy
John R. Wooden Certified Coach, Coaching Success Curricula

INTRODUCTION

I've been fascinated by leadership for a very long time. I've read and studied it, and I've worked for good leaders and a few poor ones. I opened a business in 2000 thinking I knew what I needed to know about being the leader of my own business; I could not have been more wrong.

I spent the next eighteen years (barely) surviving. What I really did was trade bosses. I became my own boss, but I wasn't a true leader of my business. I made all the fundamental mistakes that lead to failure. I borrowed money from family and friends, took on bad clients who I actually knew weren't a good fit for me or my business, and worked with "friends and colleagues" who were fundamentally opposed to what I was trying to accomplish and were undermining me without my realizing it. Again, it was survival, not leadership.

I finally reached a point where I knew three things had to happen…

- I had done all I could do with my old company, and it was time to end my dead-end, struggling business.
- I wanted to start a new company that allowed me to focus on things I knew I could do well, such as public speaking and mentoring.

- I needed to take what I did well and raise those skills to a higher level than they had ever been before; I needed to study some of the top leaders in the areas I was interested in. I spent ten years as the chair of the New York City Disability Mentoring Day program, and now I needed to be mentored myself.

The first section of this workbook encompasses the long, winding, and amazing journey I've taken. Not only have I had the pleasure of studying from some of the great leaders and speakers of our time—such as John Maxwell, Brian Tracy, Jack Canfield, and the teachings of the greatest coach who's ever lived, John Wooden—but I was also privileged to have them take an interest in me and help me achieve goals I never would have believed possible, not the least of which is becoming a leadership and mentoring coach. I will discuss my own experience with being coached and how it completely altered my thought process and ultimately led me to become a professionally certified coach.

The second section of the book is designed to help you as the leader of your business examine your own leadership skills, dive deeply into your leadership development, and finally, inspect your overall health as a leader and how your leadership skills have affected your business development. This section contains ninety-seven questions (not a typo) that are divided into the three parts mentioned above.

At the end of the book, I'll help you identify how coaching might benefit you based on your answers to the ninety-seven questions, and finally, present you with a very special offer I hope you'll take advantage of. It may make a similar impact on you as it did me. As John Maxwell says, "Everything rises and falls on leadership."

I wish you the best of luck as you begin to use the tools in this book. Let's get started.

THE BENEFITS OF COACHING

The great myth about leadership is people think it's easy. They think their bosses have it made, make more money, control their schedule, control the lives of employees...

Please allow me to share a secret. With the sole exception of controlling your own schedule, being the leader of your business is one hundred times more difficult unless you have several million in the bank and are able to run your business as a hobby.

There are at least ten reasons why this is so, but I'll only highlight one. As an employee, your salary is guaranteed. As the leader of your business, you are the person responsible for generating the revenue. Once the bills are paid, you may or may not have enough money left to pay employees or, better yet, yourself.

I've lived this situation myself, and I did so for many years. It's no fun. It can cost money, friendships, marriages, and self-esteem. The worst part is that leaders become so locked into the day-to-day aspects of keeping the business running at any cost, they can lose all perspective.

I finally reached that point with my last company and decided to try something new that was much more aligned with my strengths. I was not overly worried about getting the training and education I would need to become a certified speaker, trainer, and coach. What concerned me more was making sure I wouldn't repeat my past mistakes as the leader of my business. I was determined to avoid that trap. Working with a coach seemed like the answer. It was! Over several months, the impact of coaching for me has been amazing. It has literally changed my entire thought process for my new business and is now a primary reason I've become a certified leadership and mentoring coach myself.

As I have reviewed and analyzed the benefits of business and leadership coaching for me and my company, there are five that stand out.

- Through coaching, I realized I need people to help me build and run my business effectively. The idea that every entrepreneur must be able to do every single job and perform all these roles effectively is not only a myth—it's a way to almost guarantee failure. It's imperative I'm able to perform the tasks I do well that will generate revenue for the business. As the leader, I'm responsible for making sure that all key functions of the business are being handled correctly. At the same time, I need to assign and delegate those tasks to people more qualified than I am to perform them well.
- My coach helped me rethink my overall goals for the business. She asked me pointed questions that were designed to help me expand my vision and explore different possibilities, and she worked with me to readjust the planning process once decisions were made.
- The coach held me accountable. Goals and objectives were set for each week's session. It helped me organize, prioritize, and even remove the distractions that inevitably occurred as my launch plan took shape.
- My coach was always honest and objective, even though she knew some of her thoughts and suggestions might make me

uncomfortable. A good coach will help guide you toward the best answer.

- Coaching is coaching. Not consulting, mentoring, or therapy. It is designed to find solutions for the client. The best coaches do this by helping the client find the solution from within themselves.

The beauty of coaching is that anyone can benefit from it. Leadership coaching is especially critical for professionals who are looking to grow their businesses. I wish I had worked with a coach years ago. Had I made that smart, simple investment, I'd have been much more successful than I was as the leader of my previous business.

I have good news for you. Once I learned how coaching could help me, as well as any business owner, I became dedicated to becoming a professional business coach myself. Through much study, I have learned from some of the world's top coaches and have grown into a coach that can help you thrive.

MY PROCESS OF BECOMING A PROFESSIONAL SPEAKER, TRAINER, AND COACH

About a year ago, I was putting the finishing touches on my book, *The Art of Mentoring Workbook*, which describes my long-standing involvement with mentoring based on my own experience as the chair of the Disability Mentoring Day program in New York City and being mentored growing up with a physical disability. I was also preparing to go to Orlando to receive my professional certification as a John Maxwell speaker, trainer, and coach. Once that happened, I would be able to begin a speaking business based on the Maxwell teaching on leadership.

This was a career change. I was going through a divorce, and I had also decided that after twenty years of service to the disability community I am part of, I had done all I could and needed something new and different that also matched my enjoyment and ability to speak and coach.

First, I attended the Maxwell convention in Orlando, a five-day event. In order to complete the certification process, one of the requirements was to give a "table speech" to my peers at the table I was assigned to. The rules stated I had to choose a topic, after which I would have five minutes and twenty-five seconds to give my speech. I could be within thirty seconds either way of the time limit to pass. As it turned out, I was the last person to give the speech at my table... and I hit the 5:25 time limit exactly.

After my peers voted me as the best speaker and potential coach at the table—an amazing honor—the Maxwell faculty noticed me and offered me a chance at further and more sophisticated training within their organization and an opportunity to potentially join their ranks. The main reason for this was they wanted to make an introduction for me to meet with renowned speaker and author Brian Tracy and attend his speaking academy.

It didn't thrill me to postpone my launch, and the speaking academy was expensive, but ultimately, the opportunity was too good to pass on. Besides, I had read several of Brian Tracy's books over the years and was anxious to meet him. So even though this opportunity would delay my new business's launch, I went to San Diego to attend Brian's event.

After three days of intense learning and speaking from a true master, I received the certification as a graduate of the Brian Tracy Speaking Academy. Brian and I had hit it off, and at the end of the academy, he pulled me aside and encouraged me to keep pursuing this, to become one of the best. After hearing his words, I knew it was what I wanted—to go the extra mile and work to become a top of the line speaker and coach.

As a graduate of the Brian Tracy Speaking Academy, I had access to his vast library of information and teaching, which allowed me to continue adding to my knowledge base and work with one of his private coaches. I quickly realized that to become a top-notch speaker and coach, I needed to learn more than I knew, and working with a coach seemed like a good idea.

I began working with my coach, which further impressed on me the benefits of having a professional coach. She eventually asked me if I would be content teaching someone else's material when I had the ability to teach my own. What she was suggesting was a complete game changer for me. It allowed me to expand my horizons; even though this would push back my business launch a little further, I was determined.

Enter Jack Canfield. As it turned out, Brian Tracy and Jack Canfield had an affiliation within their coaching businesses, which turned out to be a stroke of luck for me. Through my participation at the speaking academy, I was invited to receive another training and certification from Jack Canfield. This particular certification involved teaching his success principles.

After hard work over several weeks and months and getting through his crash study program, my knowledge base had probably now increased five times beyond what I knew when I attended the Maxwell conference in Orlando. Additionally, Jack Canfield offered me the opportunity to receive further coach training.

After this, I was contacted by the International Coach Federation and asked to join their membership and take a course to certify as a professional coach. Along with that, I was invited to receive an extremely rare certification to teach the great coach John Wooden's amazing leadership and mentoring material through his world-famous Pyramid of Success. All of this amazing training from the top coaches and teachers of leadership, mentoring, and success gave me the opportunity to completely change my business model and teach all of the above, along with my own original material from the perspective and knowledge of a professionally certified coach.

I'm proud of the fact that despite launching my company a full year after I planned, I was able to build a business with more potential and ability to help people than I ever could have imagined. I learned the value of flexibility and adaptability. These are vitally important skills for the leader of any business, enhancing the capability to achieve business and leadership growth. I'm living proof that coaching can change your company and you, yourself, as a leader.

YOU ARE A PROFESSIONAL, BUT ARE YOU A GOOD LEADER FOR YOUR BUSINESS?

As I was going through all of my training and education, I realized the question above is a *key* question that can determine if your business will be successful or not! If you're not a good leader for your business, more than likely, your business will not be nearly as successful as it could be or fail entirely. If I were to rate myself as a leader from one to five (lowest to highest) for my previous company, I would give myself a two. Had you asked me that question two years ago, I would have said four. But two is the correct answer. I made several key mistakes that created obstacles to growth and success.

- I tried to complete every task myself instead of delegating the ones I wasn't particularly good at. In other words, I got in my own way.
- Despite being part of the community I was selling my services to, I was not selling to the right customers. I also took on clients who were terrible fits for me and my company.
- I failed to put systems in place that would allow the company to run smoothly and allow me to focus on what I needed to grow the business.

There were others, but you get the idea. Does any of this sound familiar? If so, don't worry—help is on the way!

Here's how the coaching process starts to develop. In the sections that follow, you'll find some key leadership evaluation questions. Before answering these, rate yourself as the leader of your business. As you read, answer (very honestly) how you rate in those areas. Once done, go back and reevaluate yourself as the leader. If the score is now lower, that's great! What you have done successfully is identified areas where improvement can be achieved. The score you gave yourself means nothing. The key is always striving for improvement, and this is where coaching becomes a vital tool for any leader looking to build and grow a business.

THE CRITICAL DIFFERENCE BETWEEN COACHING AND MENTORING, AND THE VALUE EACH PROVIDES TO A BUSINESS OWNER

It may seem hard to believe these two useful disciplines would need further definition or clarification, but too often I've seen them overlap; when they do, the effectiveness of both diminish.

Using the example below, let's illustrate the differences very clearly so we can see what professional coaching can bring you.

A small business owner feels overwhelmed. She is a one-person operation with two part-time employees. She worked in the telecommunications industry for twelve years and has now opened her own consulting business, which specializes in helping large companies manage their teleconferencing and internet-based communications. She has two full-time clients and weekly deadlines to meet. Her clients make their payments within about thirty to forty-five days of invoice, so she occasionally has to pay her employees from her personal account. Between her weekly deadlines and tight cash flow, she has very little time to market her business, network with other professionals, or attract new clients. More than once, her clients have asked her to drop what she is doing and focus on a specific issue or project they have upcoming, and when this happens, she often falls behind on her deliverables. Her days are getting longer, and her productivity is down. She is looking for help and advice and has begun to question how much longer she can do this…

COACH – The coach's job is to help the client find solutions that come from within themselves. Here are a few questions a good coach may ask…

- What can you do to get your clients to pay faster?
- What can you delegate to your employees so you can meet your deadlines?
- Do you keep a list of tasks to be prioritized on a daily and weekly basis? It might keep you from feeling overwhelmed.
- Could you assign someone to go to marketing or networking events in order to increase business?

MENTOR – The mentoring role consists of sharing experience and assisting in professional growth and development. A mentor might make the following statements and suggestions…

- I was in this very same situation when I began my business. These are some things I did that helped me alleviate my situation.
- Why don't you come by the office and spend a day watching how I do what I do? If you'd like, we can devote an afternoon or so each week to go over things.
- There is a group I meet with over lunch every other week to discuss these same challenges you're facing. I'll sponsor you and pay for your first two months of membership.

- I may not have an answer for this problem, but I know someone in your industry who can help you. Let me make an introduction for you.

Here is a quick exercise: go back to the top of this article. Take sixty seconds and look at the coaching questions. Then do the same for the mentoring statements. It should become clear pretty quickly that each role provides its own important value but should not intermingle with the other. The coach is fully focused on professionally guiding clients to enhance their leadership skills and business plan using their own strengths.

How Each Relationship Should Progress

One of the most important things to remember is that steady progress should be expected as time goes by. Going back to our example above, here are some distinguishing differences between coaching and mentoring when it comes to progression.

COACH – Here are some questions and statements a coach might leave with a client as one session ends and preparation for the next one begins...

- Let's highlight the key points from today's session.
- What are the takeaways from our discussion?
- What can you do this week to alleviate some of the issues you are dealing with?
- Please chart your progress and send it to me twenty-four hours before our next session.

- What are you accountable for this week? What are your employees accountable for?

MENTOR – A mentor is usually more directly involved with the person they are mentoring. Given the difference, the questions and statements would be more along these lines...

- Let's make sure we meet at least twice this week, so we can work on finding the solution together. I'll have some ideas and suggestions ready.
- After we meet, let's exchange emails with ideas we can go back and forth on. We can set up an additional meeting later in the week if we need to.
- I'm available at all times if you need to chat and talk about the progress you've made. If you're frustrated, we can certainly explore other solutions together as well.
- I was going through some old notes from a few years ago when I had this same problem. This is what I did, and I'm sure it will help you.
- There's a lecture this week that discusses a lot of the problems you're having. I know the person who's speaking. Why don't we go together, and I'll see if I can't arrange for some private time for you with him when it's over?

Again, the difference is clear. Both roles can be very important and useful to a business owner. By keeping the roles separate and distinct, you'll have built in tools from different perspectives that will provide excellent resources and support as you build your business. Mentors are wonderful to have, but I've found that having my own coach was an incredible investment that changed my business and me as a leader.

THE FOUNDATION OF LEADERSHIP EXCELLENCE

At this point in our discussion, let's focus on getting to know you as a leader. The questions below will help identify what I like to call your leadership compass. As a coach, it naturally identifies the correct starting point when I work with a client. Go to it!

1. Do you possess a good leadership attitude? Write three examples.

2. What is your leadership mindset?

The Ultimate Leadership Workbook

3. Do you enjoy being the leader of your business? If so, why?

4. Do you believe you are a leader worth following? Explain.

5. Are you a business owner who is simply an employee of your business? Detail why you feel this way:

7. Are you comfortable and confident as a leader? If so, why?

8. Are you at your best as a leader when your best is needed? Give three examples:

9. Do you feel prepared as a leader to handle any and every situation that may arise? Give three examples.

Leadership excellence is something we all strive for. We also know that achieving this excellence is an ongoing process that never ends. Speaking for myself, I've never met a perfect leader. I do believe what my friend Brian Tracy has said many times: "Leaders are made, not born." There are many books on leadership. I've read a lot of them, and what I've learned over the years is that you can study leadership forever (and you should), but it takes a lot of hard work to become an excellent leader. If that sounds daunting, this next statement will be even more so—it takes hard work every single day. As I continue my own ongoing evolution as a leader and leadership coach, it becomes very clear that creating the foundation of leadership excellence in any business or profession begins with leaders asking themselves the questions below.

1. What can you do more of to increase your efficiency and effectiveness?

3. Do you possess the basic skills of an effective leader? List them:

4. Do you, as a leader, show flexibility and adaptability as needed and warranted? How?

5. Do you gather information effectively? How?

6. Are you a detail-oriented leader? Give three examples:

7. Are you giving your best efforts to your business, employees, and customers each day? How do you achieve this?

8. Do you as a leader work effectively? Explain how:

These questions will allow you to begin analyzing yourself as a leader. Remember that becoming a truly effective leader involves growth, self-awareness, and a willingness to change. Effective coaching can help expedite the process and thus achieve faster results that lead to self-improvement, business goals, and improved relationships with employees and clients.

ANALYZING YOURSELF AS A LEADER

The hard work now begins. The questions below will define where you are as a leader right now. They go right to the heart of personal leadership. As your coach, I'd like to offer some words of encouragement. These are questions that every leader in any profession must ask themselves regularly. There are no wrong answers. The idea is to become a better leader who will work to grow and improve your business. If you take the time to give complete, thoughtful, and—above all—honest answers, growth and improvement will happen.

1. What is your greatest leadership challenge?

2. What are your three greatest strengths as a leader?

3. What are your three biggest weaknesses as a leader? What can be done to improve on them?

4. What are the specific skills you need to improve on as a leader (name three)?

5. Are you afraid of failure? Do you learn from it? List three instances:

6. What can you do to enhance your well being as a leader?

7. What as a leader would you like to accomplish now, in three months, six months, and a year?

8. Do you do an evening review of your day as the leader of your business? What aspects does it include?

9. Do you take time to read books about and study leadership? About your industry or profession? List three books you have read recently:

10. Do you evaluate your own performance as a leader on a weekly or monthly basis? What aspects do you cover?

11. Have you ever worked with a leadership coach? List the challenges you'd like to overcome with a leadership coach.

THE DAILY CHALLENGES OF LEADERSHIP

These questions are where effective leadership is truly brought into focus. The leader who handles the daily challenges well is on their way to building a successful business. Full disclosure from your coach—this was my weakest area of leadership for years. It's very easy to allow yourself to become distracted and lose focus on what you need to be doing as the leader. This is especially true if you work in a home or noisy work setting, when your spouse or kids want or need something, or when you see something on the news or receive a text. There are instant distractions everywhere!

Studies have shown that each interruption or distraction causes you to lose twenty minutes of work time. In simple math, elimination of three distractions per day equals one extra hour of productivity per day. Multiply that by five days per week, then four weeks in a typical month, and you have twenty extra hours. This is the equivalent of three plus extra business days to grow your business without adding a single hour of time to your work schedule! So let's eliminate all distractions as you answer these questions.

1. Do you manage your time effectively? How do you do this?

2. Do you have a daily plan as the leader of your business? Explain how this works:

3. List your three most important tasks each day, for the week:

4. Do you keep a daily calendar? Weekly?

5. Do you say no to people and projects that cause you to lose focus or distract you from what you need to do? List three instances where you have said no:

6. What could you do as the leader of your business that would allow you to focus 25% more time on your greatest strengths?

7. Do you set aside "think time" for your business? If so, how long, and when?

8. Do you have the ability to really focus on your business tasks over the course of your day? How do you manage this:

9. What can you delegate to your staff that you aren't as of now? Conversely, what must you, and only you, do as the leader of your business?

10. What tasks might you delegate to your staff that could save you one hour per day?

11. What is your process for eliminating distractions?

USING YOUR ENHANCED LEADERSHIP TOOLS TO DEVELOP YOUR COMPANY TO ITS FULL POTENTIAL

Congratulations on coming this far! You're making great progress toward your goal of becoming the best leader of your business that you can be. Let's now turn our attention to using your enhanced leadership skills and mindset to grow your business. I'm willing to bet you'll see things with a very clear focus as we move forward.

We'll be using the exact same techniques to analyze your business development skills. One of the best ways to lead, sell, and develop anything is to ask important questions. The answers to the questions below should be crystal clear to you, the leader. If they aren't, then these questions have instantly diagnosed a major problem that should be addressed immediately.

1. What are your company's core products and services?

2. What is your company's purpose?

3. Are you familiar with the trends in your industry or profession?

4. What could you as a leader change about your industry?

5. Is your business systems oriented? How so?

6. Is your business systematic? Detail:

7. Do you use the 80/20 principle for your business? This means spending 80% of your time on the 20% of your business that makes it successful. Explain:

8. What does your company do exceptionally well? List three aspects:

9. What does your company do poorly that could possibly be eliminated? List three aspects:

THE PLAN FOR GROWTH

We've spent a lot of time so far on leadership, leadership development, and company development. We are now about to enter what is arguably the most important part of being the leader of your business—the plan for growing your company so it can become extremely successful. Like everything else in business, a plan is needed, and there must be a process to execute that plan. Using what we've worked on and what you have learned so far, begin working on the set of questions below. Please allow me to do a little coaching here. I would strongly advise you to handle these questions in a three-part process:

- First, take as much time as you need to answer these questions yourself in your leadership position. Dive deeply into each of the questions as you arrive at your answers.
- Once this is done, expand the circle and include your key employees, advisors, and so forth; share your conclusions and ask for input. It may be worthwhile to let these key people answer the questions themselves.
- Create a growth plan and execute!

1. What do you do on a daily and weekly basis to grow your business? List three:

2. What is the "planning process" for your business? Do you regularly engage in it?

3. Do you have a strategic plan for the business (different from a business plan)?

4. What is your goal setting process for your business? What are your short-, medium-, and long-term goals for your business?

5. How were the goals you set determined?

6. Has your company consistently met the goals you've set forth over time? Give specifics:

7. Have you set clear priorities for your business? Are they set in order of importance? List them:

8. Are you alert to new opportunities for business growth? How do you achieve this?

9. Are you open-minded to pursuing new concepts and processes for your business? Why do you think this is important?

10. Have you planned for the growth and development of your business carefully enough?

AN ESSENTIAL LEADERSHIP SKILL: EFFECTIVE COMMUNICATION

The ability to communicate effectively with your employees and clients is crucial to your success as the leader of your company. Failure to communicate equals failure to succeed. In the business climate we have today, it really is that simple! As a coach, I've found this skill is often an issue, and even a barrier, for leaders. I also realize that some leaders are natural introverts who prefer to focus on their tasks at hand and work behind closed doors. I will make the argument here that if that's your preferred leadership style, that's okay. You don't have to change your leadership style to become a good communicator.

What you must do to communicate effectively as the leader of your business is the following:

- Make sure your goals, objectives, and expectations are in line with those of your employees. You should set the goals. Make sure you have buy-in from the employees. Also, make sure you provide the tools needed for success.
- Listen carefully to your employees' questions and concerns.
- Be open-minded to suggestions. It may be possible that someone closer to the "ground floor" may know something you don't.

- Provide constructive feedback, both good and bad, to your employees.

The points above also apply when dealing with clients.

The questions in this section are key cogs in the growth process of your business. Think of a grandfather clock and how it works. All the different pieces work in harmony to create a great symmetry that keeps everything running smoothly and on time. Answering these questions honestly and getting important feedback from employees and clients will help your business clock run with great precision and effectiveness.

1. Are you an open-minded leader? If so, explain why. If not, explain why.

2. Do you consider yourself a good listener? Do you actively listen to your staff and clients? List three examples:

3. Are you an effective communicator? Would your employees and clients agree?

4. What do you do well as a communicator? Do you execute? Do you get results? Give three examples:

5. What are your strengths (name three) as a communicator?

6. What are your weaknesses (name three)? How can you improve on these?

[   ]

These questions are extremely important, but communication is only one element of your connections with those you work with. Next, we'll discuss in detail the importance of developing healthy relationships with your employees and clients.

LEADING YOUR EMPLOYEES

We have already discussed how important it is to have people you can rely on to help you build your business. You as the leader are responsible for putting them into the right position to succeed and molding them into an effective team. In order to do that successfully, you must, as their leader, get them to buy into your vision for your business's growth and development. The questions below will help you evaluate your leadership skills in this area. It may also help you figure out what your employees' strengths and weaknesses are, where to best utilize them, and even whether or not they are a good fit for your business.

This is an area for me that is in constant development. I'd advise you to give a lot of time and thought into this set of questions. All of us as leaders have struggled with this part of leadership. Many headaches can be saved if the right people are in place.

1. Do you trust your staff to complete their tasks effectively each day? Give examples:

2. Do you set realistic goals for yourself and your employees? What can you as a leader do to help them reach their goals?

3. Are you a championship team builder? How so?

4. Are you a teacher? Give three examples:

5. Are you utilizing your employees correctly, making the most of their strengths? How so?

THE VALUE OF MENTORING AS PART OF LEADERSHIP

Mentoring is an area I'm very familiar with. To hear about my own experience, please read my book, *The Art of Mentoring*. With that shameless plug out of the way, let's discuss why mentoring is a very important part of good leadership.

- Mentoring is a great way to develop your employees and help them add value to your business over the long term.
- Mentoring is a great way to create "buy-in" since your employees will see their development and career goals matter to you as their leader.
- Mentoring can create long-term relationships that can be very valuable to your company. It's simply good business.

As you think about the value of mentoring for your company, keep something in mind: you weren't always a leader. Becoming one is an accomplishment to be proud of. Think about whoever it was who helped you and guided your career. Would you have been able to become the leader of your business without that guidance and support? An investment in mentoring is an investment in your company and its continued growth and success. An employee who feels they have a real opportunity to succeed will come to work happy and enthusiastic. Attitude is everything!

1. Do you have a mentoring and skills development program for your business? Do you invest in education for your staff?

2. Name two or three people within your organization who you might be willing to mentor.

   a. What are their strengths and weaknesses?

b. What could you as their mentor do to help them achieve their career goals and objectives?

c. If you effectively mentor these people, do you see them as long-term assets for your business?

d. How, as their mentor, can you help them develop their skills?

e. As you are working with your best employees and developing them, what future role(s) could you see for them within your organization?

3. Do you prepare your staff to be confident in their role(s) at your company?

4. Do you practice the three Rs (reward, recognition, and reinforcement) with your employees?

5. How often do you meet with your staff to discuss performance? Are you familiar with their goals and objectives?

6. How would your mentee(s) evaluate your skills and leadership qualities?

SETTING THE TONE OF SUCCESS

When it comes to setting a tone of success for a business, there is good news and bad news for the leader. The bad news is tone is not tangible. You can't see or feel tone. The good news is this is an area the leader can make a direct impact on. If the leader sets the right tone for the business, then he or she can create a tangible RESULT.

Here's more good news—this is a very coachable process for a leader. If this is worked on correctly, I can almost guarantee improvement in a fairly short period of time. I say this because attitude, loyalty, and cooperation with others are behaviors that the leader can control directly. If the leader has control over the outcome, it's firmly in his or her hands to make sure the desired outcome is achieved. Good coaching can help.

To get an idea of the current tone of your business, answer the questions below. It may also be a good idea to get honest and thoughtful feedback from your staff. Keep in mind before you start that if you ask for honest feedback, you just might get it. That's a good thing. How you respond to what you hear will say a lot about your leadership and the kind of tone you set for the company. It may not be easy to hear, but it could be a critical moment for your company's future if handled well.

1. Have you created a positive company culture? Explain how:

2. Do you believe your people are happy and even excited to come to work every day? How do you know?

3. Do you believe your attitude affects your staff and their ability to get things done?

4. Do you believe your staff thinks you're a leader worth following?

5. Are you loyal to your support staff? Conversely, do you feel your staff is loyal to you as their leader?

6. Does your staff consider you approachable? Give three examples:

7. Are you cooperative with your staff and clients? Give three recent examples:

8. Do you as a leader inspire your staff? How do you achieve this?

9. What do you do to keep your employees motivated?

10. Do your personal feelings about staff members and clients affect your judgment at times in the professional setting of your business? Do you maintain your poise in difficult situations or when it's needed most? Give three examples:

11. What are two basic needs for each member of your staff?

LEADING THE HEART OF THE BUSINESS: YOUR CLIENTS

There are two parts to consider when it comes to what I refer to as leadership of your clients. Both are critical to success and failure, and they are controlled by the leader. The first is the truth that leading your clients is the single most important component of your business. Without your clients, you have no business. Take a good hard look at the questions below and make sure you have the right answers.

1. How would you evaluate your customer service? Would your clients answer differently?

2. What are two basic needs of your clients?

3. What can you do to enhance your best clients' experience with your company?

4. Would your customers buy from you again?

5. Do you operate with ethics and integrity? Do your clients believe you do?

6. Are you considered a "go to" person in your industry by your clients?

7. Do your clients enjoy working with you? Have you asked them?

The next point to consider about clients is a difficult one to think about. An undervalued but critical part of leadership is keeping the best clients and firing the bad ones.

The above statement may seem ridiculous at first glance, not to mention counterintuitive. Every single business owner needs as many clients as they can possibly get, right?

Right... EXCEPT the wrong ones. Now here's something even more counterintuitive. By the wrong clients, I'm not necessarily referring to people who don't need your services.

Unfortunately, I have vast experience in this area. The circumstances of life and marriage caused me to take on clients that were waving checks at me. It (temporarily) solved my immediate money issues. There were only five problems:

- They were not the kind of clients that advanced the goals and objectives of my company.
- They were not long-term clients, so repeat business was highly unlikely.
- The money they paid me was not concurrent to the many hours needed to do the necessary work.
- They were unpleasant, difficult, dishonest, and since one of them was "family," they had no qualms about taking advantage of me (calling at any and all hours of the night, demanding I go well above and beyond what anyone would consider reasonable service).
- They had very little money.

The fault lies with me. I, as the leader, allowed my former company to go off the rails for one very simple reason: I took on clients who paid my immediate bills but destroyed my business, not to mention my marriage, my financial stability, and my self-esteem. The worst part is that, subconsciously, I knew what I was doing and didn't put a stop to it.

I want to help leaders who are in the same position I was avoid the mistakes I made. We all have or have had clients who are not good for us or our businesses. Conversely, we all have clients that have helped our businesses grow and prosper. As simple as it sounds, one of the key functions a leader must concentrate on is to focus and nurture their best clients and get rid of (I *did* say get rid of) the bad ones. Fast!

The exercise below is one of the most important a leader can do. It should be done at least every quarter. Take two sheets of paper. On one sheet, list your best clients. On the other, list your most difficult clients. Here are some key questions to ask as you go along.

- Does the client pay? On time? (Anyone can run into a cash crunch. It happens. When it becomes chronic, a red flag should go up.)
- Once you have completed your work for the client, will they come back? (Otherwise known as repeat and recurring revenue.)
- How much revenue does this client add to your bottom line?
- Is this client a prototype for your company?
- Are they pleasant to work with?
- Do they communicate effectively with you and do you do the same with them?
- When issues have arisen, has this client worked well with you to resolve them? (If not, I'd advise you to get rid of them quickly. Troublemakers cause trouble for the fun of it.)

- Will this client potentially refer others to you?
- Do you have a history with this client? (It's always a good idea to be extra loyal whenever possible to a client of long-standing.)

These are vital questions to the overall health of your business. As the leader, you are obligated to yourself and your team to make sure you come up with the right answers to these questions. They are not always easy to answer, but they are *crucial*. By not answering them properly, I failed as a leader when I ran my last company. I don't want to see that happen to you. Please send me an email or drop me a line if you are struggling with this process. I've been there, and I can help. Good luck!

Now, here are questions for *you* in order to analyze how you operate with clients. Remember—answer honestly!

1. Do you interview your clients before you work with them? What questions do you ask?

2. Are you working with the right clients for your business?

3. List your five best clients. What makes them your best clients?

4. How do you avoid the wrong ones?

5. How many of the wrong type of clients are you currently involved with? Can these relationships be fixed? If not, what's your strategy to remove them from your business?

6. What can be done to enhance relationships with your clients?

CONCLUSION: NOW YOU SEE WHY THIS IS A WORKBOOK

I really want to commend you for putting in so much hard work. It's gratifying for a coach to work with a leader who shows such commitment to leading their business. It's an honor. The questions here are designed to accomplish two things:

- Provide the leader with a very clear picture of where they stand with their individual skills and as the leader of their business.
- Provide a clear diagnostic tool that shows the leader and company's strengths and the areas that need improvement.

As you go through your answers, try and narrow down your focus to the areas you as the leader of your business feel are the most important to work on. Pick your top three.

The diagnostic tool is also used for me. It helps me figure out how I can help you as a coach to continue your leadership journey. If you submit your answers to me, I will do two things for you:

- I will provide a free thirty-minute coaching session for you.
- I will create a coaching plan we can use together to continue working on the areas of your choice.

Remember, even though we have reached the end of the workbook, the real work of improving your personal and professional leadership is just beginning. It will go a lot faster and be so much easier with the help of a coach. I have been in leadership for decades. It's not an accident that when I began the year-long process of building my company, working with a coach made me realize how much I needed to learn in order to become a truly successful leader as a business owner and as a coach of leadership and mentoring. Without being coached myself, I promise you would have never seen this workbook. Good coaching can make a major difference in the degree of success you achieve as the leader of your business.

But I'm not done yet…

As a gift to you, for reading this book, I will offer an additional thirty minutes of coaching time and an opportunity to join my private inner circle at a 10% discount. This, along with the workbook you've just completed, will give you maximum opportunity to develop and improve your business leadership skills. To access this special offer, visit my website, www.jtdcoaching.com, where you'll find more about how we can connect. I would love to help you reach the business goals you've always dreamed about.

I'm rooting for you as a leader. It takes courage to own and run a business; it can be lonely and difficult. It's also incredibly rewarding and gratifying when it succeeds. I'm here to help, and I look forward to working with you in the future. To your great success!

NOTES

Eric Jackier

Eric Jackier

Eric Jackier

www.ingramcontent.com/pod-product-compliance
Lightning Source LLC
Chambersburg PA
CBHW081452220526
45466CB00008B/2603